Paper Artist

Creations Kids Can Fold, Tear, Wear, or Share

by Gail D. Green, Kara L. Laughlin, and Jennifer Phillips

capstone

Table *of* Contents

Chapter 3:
Classy Keepsakes

Chapter 4:
Dazzling Decorations

Fold it.
Tear it.
Share it.
Wear it.

There's simply no end to what you can do with paper. Just follow the step-by-step instructions in this book, and transform yourself into a paper craft artist. Amaze your family and friends—and even yourself—with the dramatic pieces you'll create with simple, everyday paper.

Ready to get started? As a paper artist you'll need a few supplies. First, gather paper. Magazines, newspaper, wrapping paper, maps, and sheet music are just a few unique paper sources that will bring your projects to life. Then gather craft supplies such as glue, scissors, and markers. To complete some projects in this book, you'll need to find quilling tools too. Just ask your local craft store for help if you can't find these yourself.

Paper crafts are all about letting your inner artist shine. So get going, and unfold the fun!

1 hot glue gun
2 craft knife
3 compass
4 spray paint
5 craft glue
6 decoupage glue
7 foam brush
8 quilling needle
9 slotted quilling tool

Butterfly Necklace

Let your creativity take flight with this pretty piece. It truly will be the centerpiece of any outfit.

1. Draw the outline of a butterfly that's about 3 inches (8 centimeters) wide on poster board. (If drawing isn't your thing, you can find butterfly templates online to trace.) Then cut out the butterfly shape.

2. Lightly sketch designs on the butterfly wings, such as long ovals. Carefully cut out the patterns with a craft knife.

3. Spray paint the butterfly on one side. Let dry. Then repeat on the other side.

4. Follow the directions on the can to spray the butterfly on both sides with sealant. Let dry.

5. Use the sharp point of the craft knife to cut a tiny hole in the bottom center of the butterfly's body. Thread a jump ring through the hole. Attach hanging beads to the jump ring.

6. Use the knife point to cut tiny holes in the top left and right wing tips. Thread jump rings through these holes, and use them to connect the chain to the wings.

7. Glue jewel beads to the butterfly's wings and body for added sparkle.

Materials:

white poster board

craft knife

glossy spray paint

clear acrylic gloss coating sealant

3 jump rings

hanging beads

necklace chain and clasp

craft glue

flat-bottomed jewel beads

Tip: Use a sharp craft knife to make sure the butterfly doesn't have ragged edges.

Ring Bling

Add a splash of color to any outfit with this spectacular ring, and let the fun blossom.

1. Measure the length around your finger. Add ½ inch (1 cm). This is the length of your cardboard piece. Then decide how slender or chunky you want your ring band. Cut a rectangle of cardboard in the dimensions you need.

2. Paint both sides of your cardboard piece. Let dry.

3. Brush decoupage glue over both sides of the cardboard piece, and let dry.

4. Wrap the cardboard band around your finger to get a correct fit. Hot glue the ends together, overlapping enough to create a strong seam. Let dry.

5. Use the compass to draw a 2-inch (5-cm) circle on decorative paper. Cut out the circle.

6. Use the compass to lightly draw a ½-inch (1-cm) circle in the center of the paper circle.

7. Cut the outside edge of the circle in strips, stopping at the center circle. Bend up every other strip slightly to create two layers of petals.

8. Hot glue a bead in the center of the flower.

9. Hot glue the flower to the ring.

10. Follow the directions on the can to spray the ring and flower with sealant. Let dry.

Materials:

tape measure

single-ply cardboard

small paint brushes

acrylic paints

decoupage glue

hot glue

math compass

decorative paper

1 bead

clear acrylic gloss coating sealant

Tip: For the cardboard, try coffee cup sleeves or look for decorative border rolls found in craft, party, and teacher supply stores.

Dangling Decorations

Can't find the perfect earrings? Then make them! You can use just about any kind of paper for these accessories, so get creative, and let your personality shine!

1. Punch four circles from the patterned paper. Glue together two circles with the pattern sides facing out. Repeat with the other two circles.

2. Punch four circles from the solid color paper. On each circle, make one cut from the edge to the center.

3. Brush decoupage glue on one side of each circle. Let dry. Repeat on the other side.

4. Follow the directions on the can to spray the circles with sealant. Spray one side and let dry. Then repeat for the other side.

5. Use a needle to poke top and bottom holes in the patterned circles a little bit from the edges. Poke a top hole in two of the plain circles.

6. Thread a jump ring through the hole in one of the plain circles. Then thread the jump ring through the bottom hole of a patterned circle. Repeat for the second earring.

7. Run glue on the inside edges of the slit in one of the remaining plain circles. Slide the circle over one of the attached plain circles. Repeat with the other circle on the second earring. Let the glue dry.

8. Use jump rings to attach earring hooks to the tops of the patterned circles.

Tip: If your decoupage glue includes a water-resistant sealant, you don't need to use the additional sealant.

Heads Up

Transform a plain plastic headband into a personal style statement. You'll turn heads with this paper project.

1. Measure the length of the headband and the width from the narrowest to widest points. Don't include the band's rims.

2. Draw a template on copy paper that follows the headband's dimensions and shape. If your paper isn't long enough, create two halves. Lay the template over the headband, and trim to fit.

3. Trace the template on decorative paper. Then cut out the shape.

4. Brush glue on the headband. Lay the decorative paper piece on top, smoothing out any wrinkles. Let dry.

5. Glue ribbon to the edges of the headband. Make sure to fold the ribbon over the edge and glue it on the back too. Let dry.

6. Insert a paper strip into the slotted quilling tool. Hold the tool with your dominant hand, and rest the tool on your other hand's forefinger. Roll the tool to quill the paper. When you get to the end, hold the rolled strip securely using your thumb and middle finger. Push the paper roll off the tool.

7. Use the quilling needle to apply glue to the rolled paper end. Press and hold until secure.

8. Repeat steps 6–7 to make as many quilled shapes as you want. Be creative with the shapes. Some can be rolled completely. Roll just part of some strips, leaving a tail. Squeeze a rolled circle to create a teardrop. Keep some rolls tight, and let others get loose before gluing. Have fun!

9. Squeeze a small puddle of glue onto scrap paper. Carefully dip the bottom edges of a shape in glue. Place the shape on the headband. Gently press down on the shape to secure. Repeat for all the shapes.

10. Glue beads or jewels to the headband as accents.

11. Follow the directions on the can to spray the headband with sealant. Let dry.

Materials:

measuring tape

wide, plastic headband

copy paper

decorative paper

foam brush

craft glue

ribbon

quilling paper strips

slotted quilling tool

quilling needle

small beads or jewels

clear acrylic gloss coating sealant

Sassy Skirt

Don't toss out that skirt! Refresh its look, and design your own boutique fashion with pretty paper rosettes.

Materials:

crepe paper streamers

scalloped edge scissors

needle and thread

clear acrylic gloss coating sealant

skirt

hot glue

beads

1. Cut a 19-inch (48-cm) length of crepe paper off the roll. Cut the paper in half lengthwise using decorative-edge scissors.

2. Thread a needle, and knot one end. Gently sew a line of stitches along the straight edge of one paper strip. Pull the thread tight as you go to create an accordion fold.

3. When you reach the end, stitch the strip's ends together. First sew up the ends, then stitch back down so the needle comes back to the stitched side.

4. Pinch the folds on the stitched side together. Run the needle through the pinched center several times to sew it together well. Knot the end of the thread and cut off the extra.

5. Pinching the stitched end, gently push the unstitched folds out flat and into a rosette shape.

6. Repeat steps 1–5 to create as many rosettes as you need.

7. Follow the directions on the can to spray the rosettes with sealant. Let dry.

8. Sew the bottom of the rosettes to your skirt. If your skirt has a built-in slip, run the needle and thread through the skirt only and not the slip.

9. Sew or hot glue beads in the centers of the flowers.

Tip: The rosettes will be water-resistant but regular washing is not recommended. Instead, use a home dry cleaning kit to clean this skirt.

Paper Purse

Keep your essentials in this fun paper purse for a day on the go. This project is so fun, you could make a new one to match every outfit!

1. Follow the directions on the can to spray both sides of the card stock sheets with sealant. Let dry.

2. Hold two card stock sheets together, pattern sides facing down. Use paper clips to keep the sheets together. Measure 1 inch (2.5 cm) from each top corner and make a mark. Then measure 2½ inches (6.4 cm) from the middle of the top edge. Make a mark there too. Draw a half circle from one edge mark to the other, with the deepest part reaching the middle mark. Cut along your pencil line. This is the top of the purse.

3. While the sheets are still clipped together, fold both sides over 1 inch (2.5 cm). Remove the clips.

4. Lay one cut sheet on your workspace, pattern side down and folded flaps standing up. Dot glue along one flap. Align the other sheet over the first sheet so the pattern side faces out. Press the flaps together, and glue in place. Repeat on the other side. Let dry.

Tip: For a different look, use a handle from an old purse instead of making a paper one.

5. Gently press the sides down to lay the purse shell flat. Fold the bottom of both sheets up 5 inches (13 cm) and crease. Unfold. Put your hand inside the purse shell and gently pop the sides back up.

6. Set the shell on your workspace with the curved top down. Gently press one bottom side in and down on the fold line. Crease the bottom flaps so they stay standing with the side pressed in. Repeat on the other side.

7. Fold the two bottom flaps in half lengthwise. Glue these flaps together as a bottom seam. Let dry.

8. Put your hand inside the purse and gently push the bottom out to sit flat.

9. To make the handle, cut two 2x12-inch (5x30-cm) strips from the third piece of card stock. On each strip, fold both long sides to the center, pattern side facing out. Apply glue underneath each fold and hold in place to dry. Overlap one end of each paper strip 1 inch (2.5 cm) and glue together. Use the craft knife to cut small holes 1 inch (2.5 cm) from each end.

10. Cut small holes on the sides of the purse, 1 inch (2.5 cm) from the top. Insert the eyelets through the holes in the handles and purse to connect them. Follow the directions with the kit to attach the eyelets. Smooth the handle into a curved shape.

11. Glue ribbon along the curved top edges to give the purse a finished look.

Pleated Flower Necklace

Head to the kitchen to get supplies for this project. Who knew baking cups could be this gorgeous?

Materials:

4 mini paper baking cups

foam brush

decoupage glue

hot glue

decorative beads and buttons

thick necklace chain

clear acrylic gloss coating sealant

1. Pinch together the bottom of a paper baking cup so the inner circle folds in tightly. Use your other hand to pull down the pleated paper edges into a circle. You can make this almost flat or keep some folds uneven.

2. Holding the folded bottom together, brush a thick layer of decoupage glue over the top pleats. Set the unglued side on a paper towel.

3. Repeat steps 1–2 with the other baking cups. Let them all dry.

4. Turn all the cups over and brush decoupage glue on the bottoms. Let dry.

Tip: Use more or fewer paper flowers on the necklace to fit your taste. It's your necklace, sc do it your way!

5. Hot glue beads or buttons in the middle of each flower. Let dry.

6. Hot glue the flowers to the necklace chain wherever you wish. Let dry.

7. Fill in the gaps between the flowers by gluing buttons on the chain.

8. Follow the directions on the can to spray both sides of the necklace with sealant. Let dry.

Lucky Stars

Make your wish for fantastic accessories come true with these shining stars. Be ready for lots of attention with these eye-catching creations.

Materials:

wrapping paper

clear acrylic gloss coating sealant

heavy sewing needle

2 1½-inch (4-cm) long earring pins
with a loop at one end

needle nose pliers

2 earring hooks

hanging beads

1. Cut two ½x12-inch (1x30-cm) paper strips.

2. Follow this folding sequence to create a star:

   - Start with one strip of paper colored side down. Tie a knot in the left end of the strip. Carefully tighten the knot.

   - There will be a short piece on the left of the knot. Tuck this piece under the top layer of the knot. The result should be a pentagon shape with a point at the top.

   - Wrap the long end of the strip tightly around and around the pentagon sides, following the natural path the paper wants to take.

   - When you have just a bit of paper left, tuck it snugly into the top layer of the knot.

   - Hold the edges of the knot between your fingers and thumbs. Use a fingernail to gently press in each side of the knot. The indented sides will cause the middle of the knot to puff up.

3. Repeat step 2 to create a second star.

4. Follow the directions on the can to spray both stars with sealant. Let dry.

5. Pierce a hole in the bottom and top point of each star with the sewing needle. Run an earring pin through each star so the loop hangs from the bottom.

6. Use a pliers to create a loop at the top of each pin and connect to the earring hooks. Attach hanging beads to the bottoms.

Tip: Practice makes perfect. Try making a few stars with plain paper before using the perfect paper for your earrings.

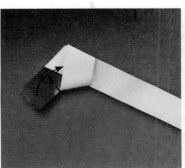
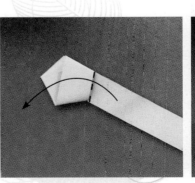
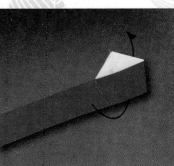

Hats Off

Top off your look with this fun crinkly hat made from tissue paper. It's the perfect accessory for your unique style!

1. Cover the hat in a tight layer of plastic wrap. Make sure the wrap follows the shape of the hat.

2. Cover just the top of the hat with a thin coating of cooking spray.

3. Brush a thin layer of decoupage glue on the sprayed part of the hat. Lay pieces of tissue paper on top of the glue, edges overlapping. Brush another thin layer of decoupage on top of the paper.

4. Continue covering the hat with tissue paper, working one small section at a time. Start by applying cooking spray to a small area. Then apply decoupage, tissue paper, then more decoupage. When finished, let the hat dry for several hours.

5. Cover the hat with another layer of tissue paper and decoupage. You don't need to use the cooking spray this time. When done, let the hat dry for several hours.

6. Repeat step 5.

7. Starting with the underside of the brim, carefully separate the tissue paper hat from the plastic-wrapped mold.

8. Follow the directions on the can to spray sealant on the hat. Let dry.

9. The hat will be pliable so you can shape it as needed. Trim the edge of the brim if needed to create a tidy look. Add a tie, yarn, or ribbon around the brim for extra flair.

Materials:

a fedora, small brimmed panama, or bowler style hat to use as a mold

plastic wrap

cooking spray

foam brush

decoupage glue

tissue paper, torn into pieces

clear acrylic gloss coating sealant

a tie, yarn, or ribbon

Belt It Out

Jazz up your outfits with a funky belt assembled from any mix of paper. Show off your wild side or go more subdued—it's up to you!

Materials:

tape measure

decorative shelf liner

decorative paper

multi-purpose spray adhesive

clear acrylic gloss coating sealant

hot glue

2 small, thin craft magnets

lightweight belt buckle or buttons

1. Measure your waist and add at least 4 inches (10 cm). This is the belt's length.

2. Decide how narrow or wide you want the belt to be. Measure the belt loops on your pants if you'll be wearing the belt that way.

3. Cut a strip of shelf liner in the dimensions you need.

4. Lay out the shelf liner with the pattern facing down. Cut strips of decorative paper that are the same width as the belt. Arrange the strips on the shelf liner. At this point, nothing will be stuck down, so you can rearrange all you want.

5. Once you're happy with arrangement, move the decorative strips off the shelf liner. Keep the strips in order so you don't forget the plan! Peel off the protective paper on the liner to expose the sticky side.

6. Use spray adhesive to attach the decorative strips to the shelf liner paper. The liner is sticky, but the adhesive gives a permanent hold.

7. Trim away any paper backing peeking out around the belt.

8. Follow the directions on the can to spray the belt with sealant. Let dry.

9. Decide what will be a comfortable fit, and hot glue the magnets to the belt's ends. Glue one magnet inside and one out, so the belt will snap closed. Hot glue a decorative belt buckle or button on the outside front.

Tip: You can use almost any type of paper for this belt. Some ideas include: mini playing cards, small gift tags, bookmarks, Chinese gift envelopes, decorative napkins, wrapping paper, play money, or book pages.

Paper Scarf

Wrap yourself in this sophisticated accessory. It looks sleek and trendy, but it's super easy to make.

Materials:

3 large 2- or 3-ply rectangular paper tablecloths in three colors

2 pipe cleaners

craft glue

clear acrylic gloss coating sealant

1. Carefully separate the layers of each paper tablecloth. Put one layer of each color on your workspace. Set the other layers aside.

2. Cut the three layers to each be 18 inches (46 cm) wide. Cut them to the length you want your scarf to be.

3. Get one of the layers you set aside. Cut two 1x12-inch (2.5x30-cm) strips from this layer. Fold each pipe cleaner inside a strip. Glue the pipe cleaner to the inside edges of the paper.

4. Lay one of the long tablecloth pieces on a flat surface. Gently roll it lengthwise into a loose cylinder. Then accordion fold it lengthwise to create soft pleats. Repeat with the other two tablecloth pieces.

5. Lay the three tablecloth pieces side by side with the ends even. Gather them together 6 inches (15 cm) from one end. Wrap a covered pipe cleaner around the layers to hold them together.

6. Loosely braid the three tablecloths together. Secure them together 6 inches (15 cm) from the other end with another pipe cleaner.

7. Follow the directions on the can to spray sealant on the scarf. Let dry.

Beaded Bracelet

Wear your heart on your sleeve! Use papers that are close to your heart to make beads for this beautiful bracelet. You'll be able to show off your personality and style all at once.

1. Cut 16 triangles from the paper. Each triangle should be 10 inches (25 cm) long and 1 inch (2.5 cm) wide on one side.

2. Put one triangle on your workspace, pattern side down. Rub glue on the triangle.

3. Put a skewer on the wide edge of the triangle. Roll the paper tightly around the stick. Glue down the tip, and slide the bead off the skewer. Repeat to create a total of 16 paper beads. If the skewer starts to get gummy from the glue, clean it off or use a new one.

4. Follow the directions on the can to spray sealant on the beads. Roll the beads to cover all sides. Let dry.

5. Thread the elastic cord through one paper bead so it's centered in the middle of the cord.

6. Thread the left end of the string through a second paper bead. Place that bead on your workspace parallel to the first bead. Both ends of the string will be on the right side.

7. Grab the string from the first bead. Put one round bead on this string. Then thread the string back through the second paper bead going left. You'll now have one string coming out both sides of the second paper bead. The round bead will create an edge between the paper beads.

8. Repeat steps 6 and 7, adding one round bead before the paper bead on the left side. Add another bead before you thread the string back over on the right side. Pull the ends tight as you work to keep the beads laying together flat.

9. When the bracelet is the length you need, add a final set of round beads on each side. Do this as you run the string ends through the first paper bead. Tie the cord's ends together in a tight knot. Cut off the extra string. Depending on the size of your wrist, you might not use all the beads or you might need more.

Materials:

decorative paper, such as sheet music, comics, maps, or your own artwork

glue stick

wooden skewers

clear acrylic gloss coating sealant

9 feet (3 meters) of elastic bracelet cord

25–30 ¼-inch (.6-cm) or larger round beads

Fancy Footwear

Take a creative stand. Turn a pair of plain shoes into fashion flair. These shoes are an accessory you can't go without.

1. Peel away the inside plain layers of the decorative napkins. Cut the decorated layers into strips.

2. Brush decoupage glue on a section of a shoe. Position a napkin strip as desired. Trim the strip if needed. Once it's the way you like, brush a thin layer of decoupage on top. Repeat in sections around both shoes until you're finished. Let dry.

3. Brush another layer of decoupage glue on the shoes. Let dry.

4. Follow the directions on the can to spray the shoes with sealant. Let them dry completely before wearing.

31

Totally Tubular Frame

Frame life's special moments with today's headlines. A picture frame crafted from newspaper pages makes a special gift everyone will treasure.

Materials:

newspaper pages

solid color paper

paper glue

rubber brayer

archival quality dye ink pads

double-sided adhesive tape

chopstick

1 6x8-inch (15x20 cm) piece of card stock

1 6x8-inch (15x20 cm) mat

1. Cut eight strips from newspaper that are 3 inches (8 cm) long by 6½ inches (17 cm) wide. Cut eight more strips from the newspaper that are 3 inches (8 cm) long by 4½ inches (11 cm) wide.

2. Repeat step 1 with the solid color paper.

3. Glue each newspaper strip to a solid paper strip of the same size. You'll have 16 double-layered strips.

4. Lay the strips newsprint side up on an extra piece of newspaper. Roll the brayer over the ink pad and then over the strips. Let dry.

5. Turn one strip so the newsprint side faces down. Apply double-sided tape along one long edge of the strip. Place a chopstick along the other long edge. Roll the strip tightly around the chopstick. Secure the taped edge to the tube when done. Then remove the chopstick. Repeat on all the strips.

6. Measure 1½ inches (4 cm) from each edge of the card stock. Cut out the center, leaving a 3 inch (8 cm) by 5 inch (13 cm) center hole.

7. Arrange the tubes along the edges of the card stock frame. Glue them in place.

8. Glue the tube frame to the mat on the side and bottom edges. Leave the top edge open to insert a photo.

9. Fold the leftover piece of card stock in half then unfold. Fold each short side back the opposite way about ½ inch (1 cm). Refold the paper on the center line. Glue the folded side pieces to the back of the mat for a stand.

Better-Than-New Vase

Vases are traditional gifts. Turn that tradition on its head with this inspiring project. The vase will be so pretty, it won't even need flowers!

Materials:

mulberry paper

foam brushes

decoupage glue

empty, clean plastic or glass vase

damp sponge

printed gift wrap, magazine pages, or decoupage paper with images that can be easily cut out

varnish

1. Hand tear 1-inch (2.5-cm) wide strips of mulberry paper.

2. Brush decoupage glue to the back of one strip. Carefully wrap the strip around the vase. Use your fingers to smooth out bubbles. Continue adding strips this way, slightly overlapping each strip, until the vase is covered.

3. Carefully wipe excess glue from the vase with a damp sponge. Press the paper down around the top and bottom of the vase to secure the edges.

4. Cut out images from printed paper. Decide how to arrange them on the vase. Apply glue to the back of each image and attach to the vase.

5. Brush two to three thin, even coats of varnish on the vase, drying between each coat.

Fluttering Butterfly Gift Bag

Make the gift bag as special as the gift. Transform a cereal box and some paper into a pretty package that will have others fluttering with excitement.

Create the bag:

1. Cut off and discard the top of the cereal box. Cut off as little or as much as you want to make the bag the size you need.

2. Glue wrapping paper to the sides and bottom of the box.

3. Lightly draw a 1x3-inch (2.5x8-cm) oval 1 inch (2.5 cm) below the top of one large side. Carefully cut out the oval. Repeat on the opposite side.

Create the butterfly:

1. Cut one 2-inch (5-cm) piece from a pipe cleaner. Cut one 4-inch (10-cm) piece from another pipe cleaner. Twist one end of the short piece around the larger piece, so the tops of both pieces are even. The pieces should make a "Y" shape. Curl the top ends of the "Y" to look like antennae.

2. Cut two 4-inch (10-cm) circles from printed paper.

3. Fold one circle in half. Then fold one corner of the folded circle toward the middle of the curved edge to form a triangle. Fold the other corner over the triangle. It should now be a multi-layered triangle with one curved edge.

4. Cut a scalloped edge on the curved edge of the triangle.

5. Open the paper back up to a circle. Cut the paper in half along the center line.

6. On one half-circle pinch the paper together on the straight edge along the fold lines. As you're pinching, push the top and bottom triangles up or down to make the whole thing look like a wing. Repeat with the other half-circle.

7. Repeat steps 3–6 with the other circle to create a total of 4 wings.

8. Hot glue the pinched point of each wing to the pipe cleaner.

9. Hot glue beads along the butterfly's body. Let dry.

10. Hot glue the butterfly to the bag.

Materials:

clean, empty cereal box

glue stick

wrapping paper

2 pipe cleaners

decorative printed paper

hot glue

decorative beads or jewels

Tip: Add an extra-special touch by using rubber stamps to decorate the outside of the bag.

Quilled Nameplate

Quilling uses paper strips and a thin tool to create amazing designs. This technique takes practice. But master it, and make some mind-blowing gifts!

1. Using an alphabet stencil, trace and cut the letters you need from a piece of solid color paper. Glue the letters across the center of the card stock.

2. Place the alphabet stencil over one of the glued letters. Hold a quilling paper strip on its edge. Curve and bend it inside the stencil to create "walls" around the letter. Carefully lift the stencil and strip together and set aside.

Materials:

block letter alphabet stencils with 2- or 3-inch (5- or 8-cm) letters

solid color paper

quick-drying paper glue with fine tip applicator

12-inch (30 cm) square sheet of heavy weight card stock

¼-inch (.6-cm) wide quilling paper strips

slotted quilling tool

quilling needle

tweezers

hole punch

ribbon

3. Place a line of glue around the outline of the flat letter. Lift the letter "wall" from the stencil. Place the bottom edge in the glue and hold in place until the glue sets. Repeat for all letters.

4. Fold one quilling strip in half width wise. Then tear it into two strips. Insert both strips into the slotted quilling tool. Hold the tool with your dominant hand, and rest the tool on your other hand's forefinger. Roll the tool to quill the paper. When you get to the end, hold the rolled strips securely using your thumb and middle finger. Push the paper roll off the tool.

Tip: When this project is done, fold up the edges of the card stock to add more dimension to the project.

5. Using the quilling needle, apply glue to the rolled paper end. Press and hold until secure.

6. Repeat steps 4–5 to create several rolled strips. Be creative with the shapes. Some can be rolled completely. Roll just part of some strips, leaving a tail. Squeeze a rolled circle to create a teardrop. Keep some rolls tight, and let others get loose before gluing. Have fun!

7. Squeeze a small puddle of glue onto scrap paper. Carefully grab a quilled shape with tweezers and dip the bottom edges in glue. Place the shape inside the walls of a letter. Gently press down on the shape with your fingers to secure. Repeat until all the letters are full.

8. Draw the outline of a simple shape, such as an oval, around the letter grouping on the card stock. Place a line of glue around the oval. Create a wall with quilling paper strips as you did in step 2 but without the stencil. Draw another oval around the first, leaving about 1 inch (2.5 cm) between them. Make a wall here too.

9. Roll more quilled shapes, and glue them between the oval walls. Let the project dry.

10. Punch holes at the top corners of the card stock square. Thread ribbon through the holes and tie to secure.

Forever Bouquet

Whether celebrating or apologizing, sometimes only roses will do. Make this awesome—and affordable—bouquet for someone special.

Materials:

1¾-inch (4.5-cm) wide crepe paper streamers

wired silk flower stems

double-sided adhesive tape

1. Cut 10 heart shapes from crepe paper. Make sure the tops and bottoms of the hearts are cut along the crepe paper roll edges.

2. Press both thumbs into the center of one heart. Pull gently with your thumbs to form a rounded petal shape. Repeat with the other hearts.

3. Cut a 4-inch (10-cm) piece of crepe paper. Loosely fold it in half lengthwise. Place a ½-inch (1-cm) strip of tape at one end of a wire stem. Loosely roll the crepe paper around the stem to form the flower center. Pinch the base of the paper, and add more tape strips as you roll.

4. Add a strip of tape around the base of the bud. Attach a petal, covering the base of the bud and squeezing the base of the petal to create a tight petal shape. Add another petal, positioned so it slightly overlaps the bud base and first petal. Continue attaching petals, one at a time, adding more tape as needed, pinching the base, and shaping the petals with your fingers.

5. Cut off a 3-inch (8-cm) section of green crepe paper. Cut two leaf shapes out. Use your thumbs to form a concave shape in these too. Use tape to attach the leaves to the flower stem just under the petals.

Swimming in Tissue

Make a scene with this spectacular present. Re-create your friend's favorite animal or activity with a tissue paper picture they can enjoy for years.

1. Measure and lightly draw lines ½ inch (1 cm) from the edges of the watercolor paper.

2. Cut two 10-inch (25-cm) and two 13-inch (33-cm) strips of tape. Attach the tape strips to the edges of the watercolor paper along your guide lines. Use the tape that hangs over to attach the watercolor paper to the bottom of a baking sheet.

3. Using a pencil, lightly draw out a scene on the watercolor paper.

4. Tear the tissue paper into multiple shapes and sizes.

5. Mix three parts glue with one part water. Brush diluted glue on the back of a tissue piece. Position the piece where needed for your scene. Smooth the tissue into place and brush the top with diluted glue.

6. Continue applying tissue paper pieces until your scene is complete. Make sure the tissue paper doesn't overlap the tape.

7. Brush a coat of glue over the entire picture. Let it dry.

8. Carefully lift the tape from the baking sheet and watercolor paper. Brush on another coat of glue to seal the image. Let it dry completely.

9. Frame the project for a professional look.

Materials:

9x12-inch (23x30-cm) sheet of watercolor paper

light-tack painter's tape

metal baking sheet

several sheets of colored tissue paper in various colors

clear craft glue

water

foam brush

picture frame

Tip: Colored tissue paper may bleed when wet. To stop colors from looking muddy, rinse your brush in clean water when changing to another color tissue.

"I Heart You" Card

A hand-written note is sometimes the best gift of all. Use your paper crafting skills to make a treasured card for someone special.

Create the heart:

1. Cut out one 3x4-inch (8x10-cm) heart from a piece of cardboard. Do the same on a piece of batting. Glue the cardboard and batting hearts together.

2. Cut one 5-inch (13-cm) square from a piece of paper. Cut several 2- and 3-inch (5- and 8-cm) squares from different papers. Glue the small squares onto the larger square in a random pattern. Overlap and angle the small squares as desired. The small squares can go over the edges of the larger one.

3. Use a marker to draw faux stitches around the edges of all the pieces.

4. Turn your paper piece upside down. Center the cardboard heart on top of the paper, batting side down. Lightly trace around the heart shape on the paper.

5. Cut the heart shape from the paper, leaving ½ inch (1 cm) extra around the entire shape. Then cut slits around the edges of the paper heart, ending each slit at the guide line. Lay the paper heart on your workspace, patterned side down.

6. Apply tape around the edges of the cardboard heart. Lay this heart, tape side up, on the paper heart. Roll the paper slits over the edges of the cardboard to stick to the tape.

Create the card:

1. Cut long strips from different paper prints in varying widths. Position the strips on the front of the folded card, overlapping the edges slightly.

2. Glue the strips in place. When they're dry, trim edges to match with the edges of the card.

3. Use a marker to draw faux stitches around the edges of the strips.

4. Glue the heart to the front of the card.

Materials:

thin cardboard

thin wool batting

paper glue

printed paper, lightweight card stock, or colorful pages from recycled sources

fine tip marker

double-sided adhesive tape

5x7-inch (13x18-cm) folded white card

Spiraling Out

Don't give the same boring magazine subscription year after year. This year turn those magazines into a creation that will surprise and inspire!

Materials:

39 magazine or catalog
pages trimmed to
7½x11-inch
(19x28-cm) sheets

large marker or highlighter

hot glue

4-inch (10-cm) cork coaster

Tip: Wrap paper strips around a squared object to create square spirals.

1. Fold one magazine sheet in half lengthwise. Open. Fold each long edge to meet the center fold. Without unfolding, fold each long edge to the center fold again. Finally fold one side over the other at the center line to create a strip that is 1 inch (2.5 cm) wide.

2. Wrap the end of the strip three-fourths of the way around a marker. Apply a thin line of hot glue along the wrapped end's short edge. Roll the strip over the glue. Hold and press until the glue is set. Continue rolling until the entire strip is completely wrapped around the marker. Glue the remaining end to the strip. Hold it until it's secure. Remove the spiral from the marker and set aside.

3. Repeat steps 1–2 to create a total of 39 spirals.

4. Hot glue three spirals onto one side of the cork coaster to create "legs" for the bowl to stand on.

5. Hot glue 12 spirals around the outside edge of the top side of the cork. The spirals should be evenly spaced. Add glue between each spiral for additional strength.

6. Create the next row by gluing 12 spirals into the spaces between the spirals in the first row.

7. Glue the last 12 spirals into a third row. Let the bowl dry completely.

Stack 'Em Up
Photo Cubes

Freeze time and celebrate special moments with this unique photo display. With all its creative combinations, this gift will never get old.

1. Cut a 3x12¼-inch (8x31-cm) piece of heavy card stock.
Then cut two 3x3½-inch (8x9-cm) pieces from card stock.

2. On the larger card stock piece, fold a tab ¼ inch (.6 cm) from
one short end. Measure 3, 6 and 9 inches (8, 15, and 23 cm) from the tab fold.
Lightly draw lines at these places. Fold the paper on these lines. The folds will create
an open-ended box. Glue the tab under the last square to hold the box together.

3. Fold ¼-inch (.6-cm) tabs on both short sides of one of the remaining card stock
pieces. Fit this piece in one of the open ends of the box. Glue the tabs inside.
Repeat with the last card stock piece.

4. Trim your photos into six 3-inch (8-cm) squares. Be creative with how you cut the
photos. For example, cut a head shot in half so you have eyes on one square and
the mouth on another.

5. Glue the photo squares onto all sides of the cube.

Sweet Owl

Whoooooo can resist this adorable gift? Stash sweet treats inside this pretty package for someone you love.

1. Glue printed paper around the outside of the toilet paper tube. Trim the paper so it lines up with the tube's edges.

2. On one end of the tube, fold the edges down, leaving two pointed sides to form owl ears. Repeat on the bottom end.

3. Cut 30 to 35 1-inch (2.5-cm) circles from decorative paper. Glue the circles around the tube, overlapping them in layers.

4. Cut two 1x2-inch (2.5x5-cm) oval wings from decorative paper. Glue to the owl body.

5. Cut one small triangle from decorative paper. Fold the triangle in half, then glue to the owl as a beak.

6. Cut two 1½-inch (4-cm) circles from white card stock. Cut two ¾-inch (2-cm) circles from printed paper. Glue the smaller circles to the larger circles. Glue wiggle eyes on the small circles. Then glue these eyes to the owl.

7. Cut a small heart from decorative paper. Glue this heart upside down behind a circle "feather" to look like feet.

8. Turn the owl upside down. Carefully open up the folded edges. Put candy inside, then re-close.

Materials:

craft glue

several sheets of decorative printed paper

empty toilet paper tube

white card stock

wiggle eyes

wrapped candy

Corrugated Bookends

Friends hold you up in times of need. Give this unique gift to remind others that you'll hold them up too!

1. Draw and cut out the shape you want from scrap paper. Your shape should be at least 6 inches (15 cm) wide and 8 inches (20 cm) tall. This will be your template.

2. Trace your template onto 12 sheets of cardboard.

3. Place one cardboard piece on a protective mat. Carefully cut out the shape with a craft knife. Repeat with the other cardboard pieces.

4. Stack 10 of the cardboard shapes. Hot glue each layer together. Rub sandpaper over the edges to make them smooth.

5. Trace your template on a map, piece of sheet music, or whatever printed paper you choose. Cut out the shape.

6. Turn your template upside down. Then trace it on the map, sheet music, or printed paper and cut out.

7. Glue one paper shape to each of the remaining cardboard shapes.

8. Hot glue the decorated cardboard shapes to the stack so the decorated sides face out.

9. Brush two coats of glaze over the entire bookend. Dry completely.

Materials:

piece of scrap paper

12 sheets of corrugated cardboard

protective mat for table surface

craft knife

hot glue

sandpaper

maps, music sheets, or printed paper

foam brush

clear, shiny glaze

Tip: Can't think of a fun shape you like? Try using the first letters of your friend's first and last names in block letters.

Box It Up

You could buy a gift box. But what's the fun in that? Make your gift extra-special with this handmade box and pleated flower.

Create the box & lid:

1. Cut an 8-inch (20-cm) square from one piece of sheet music. Cut an 8¼-inch (21-cm) square from the other piece.

2. Place the 8-inch (20-cm) square wrong side up. Fold the paper in half diagonally, then open. Repeat the fold on the opposite corners and open.

3. Fold each corner into the middle crease. Open.

4. Fold and open each corner to the fold line farthest away.

5. Fold and open each corner to the closest fold line.

6. The four squares you see in the center will be the base of the box. On one corner, cut along the two fold lines up to the corner of the base. Repeat on the opposite corner.

7. Fold the non-cut sides up along the base folds created in step 3 and down along the folds from step 2. Press the folds from step 4 out so the corners meet in the center of the base.

8. Fold the side pieces on the upright sides in toward the base along fold 3.

9. Fold up one remaining side along the fold made in step 3. Then fold it down over the side pieces along fold 2. The corner should fold out to the center of the base. Repeat with the last side.

10. Repeat steps 1-9 with the 8¼-inch (21-cm) square to create a lid.

Make a pleated flower:

1. Create small accordion folds in the paper strip. When you're done, fold the end piece over the beginning piece, and glue them together to form a crown shape.

2. Squeeze a blob of paper glue onto the card stock circle. Hold the crown with your thumbs and fingers. Press the folds so the bottom edges meet in the center to form a flower shape. This is a bit tricky, but keep trying and you'll get it.

3. Carefully place the center of the paper flower on the glue. Hold it down until dry.

4. Add hot glue to the back of a large button. Press it onto the center of the flower.

5. Hot glue the flower to the box lid.

Materials:

2 pages of sheet music or other printed paper

1x11-inch (2.5x28-cm) strip of printed paper

paper glue

1-inch (2.5-cm) circle cut from card stock

½-inch (1.3-cm) craft button with no shank

hot glue

Tip: Photo copy sheet music onto colored paper for an extra colorful touch.

Paper Tile Mosaic

Piece together a shocking gift with this paper craft project. It's just a bunch of tiny squares, but when you put them together they become so much more.

Materials:

clear craft glue

8½x11-inch (22x28-cm) photo print
or drawing

thick sheet of cardboard

magazine pages, decorated printed
paper, and solid colored papers

tweezers

dimensional resin

1. Glue the photo or drawing onto a thick sheet of cardboard. Brush a thin layer of glue on top of the entire page. Let it dry completely.

2. Cut the magazine pages and other papers into ¼-inch (.6-cm) squares.

3. Divide the paper squares into color groups.

4. Select squares that match the different color sections in your image. Using a tweezers, begin placing squares onto the image. Cut and adjust the squares where needed to fit irregular parts of the image.

5. When each section is complete, glue the squares down by picking up each square and gluing in place. Dry completely.

6. Apply dimensional resin on top of each tile to finish. Dry completely.

Tip: Use papers that have special meaning to the person who will receive the gift, such as book pages, music programs, or posters.

Handmade Stationery

Stationery is a traditional gift. Jazz up this treasured present by making the paper yourself!

Materials:

scraps of brightly colored paper, such as construction paper, napkins, or magazine pages

⅓ cup (80 mL) of dried flowers, leaves, dried herbs, fresh lavender or mint

a papermaking mold and deckle kit

large plastic container that fits the mold and deckle

several 8x10-inch (20x25-cm) white felt sheets

2 cookie sheets

sponge

1. Rip the paper scraps into small bits. You'll need 1 cup (240 mL) of paper pieces.

2. Dump the paper pieces into a blender. Add 4 cups (960 mL) of water. Place lid on blender, and blend the water/paper mixture on low for five to 10 seconds. Then blend on medium for 10 to 15 seconds.

3. Add the dried flowers, leaves, or herbs to the blender. Cover and blend on low for five to 10 seconds.

4. Place the deckle on top of the mold. Hold both frames together. Set them into a container filled with enough water to cover both frames.

5. Carefully pour the pulp from the blender into the water. Gently swish the water above the pulp to help evenly distribute the pulp on the screen. Then lift the frames straight up and allow the water to drain.

6. Gently remove the deckle by carefully lifting it off the mold. Make sure the wet paper pulp remains on the raised side of the screen.

7. Place a sheet of felt over the wet paper pulp. Be careful not to press on the wet pulp. Then quickly flip the felt, paper pulp, and mold upside down. Place the whole thing onto a cookie sheet so the felt is on the bottom and the screen is facing up.

8. Press and lightly rub a dry sponge over the screen side of the mold to remove excess water. Squeeze water from the sponge and repeat. Remove as much water as possible so the wet paper will release from the screen.

Tip: Blending the pulp for the longer times in steps 2 and 3 makes a smoother paper. The shorter times will make a textured paper.

9. Gently take the mold off the wet paper. Place a dry piece of felt on top. Place a second cookie sheet on top and press down to remove additional water. Then remove the cookie sheet.

10. Gently peel the paper off the bottom layer of felt. Place it on a dry piece of felt. Let the paper dry for 24 hours. When dry, the paper can be cut, folded, or written on—just like any paper!

Light It Up

Keep the memory of a treasured trip shining in your mind and in your room. This lamp will make any dreary day fabulous.

1. Wrap the map around the lamp shade, adjusting it so your trip route is on the shade.

2. Use a pencil to mark the map all the way around the top and bottom edges of the shade. Mark an X on the top and bottom edges where the map overlaps.

3. Draw a straight line connecting the two Xs. Then cut along your pencil marks to cut the map to fit the shade.

4. Paint a thin layer of decoupage glue on the shade.

5. Carefully wrap the cut map around the shade. Smooth out wrinkles and allow it to dry.

6. Poke earrings through the shade at places on the map where you stopped. Put the backs on the earrings to hold them in place.

7. Wrap embroidery floss around the earring posts to mark your route.

8. Cut images from travel brochures, restaurant menus, postcards, and other paper souvenirs from your trip. Brush decoupage glue on the back of each image, and press them onto the map.

9. Brush a layer of decoupage glue over the entire lamp shade. Let dry.

10. Use hot glue to attach ribbon or cord to the shade as an added decoration.

Materials:

road map

flat-sided lamp shade

foam brush

decoupage glue

post earrings with backs

embroidery floss

paper souvenirs from a trip

hot glue

ribbon or upholstery cord

Hanging Notes

Whether you like country, pop, rock, or oldies, this music-inspired wall art will rock your world.

1. Place a card stock square pattern side down on your work space. With a craft knife and ruler, score a line ½ inch (1 cm) from each side of the square. The score lines will make small squares at each corner. Cut out these squares. Then fold the card stock back along the score lines.

2. Tape inside the corners of the card stock to make an open square box.

3. Repeat steps 1–2 with the other two squares of card stock.

4. Turn the boxes patterned sides up. Glue the squares of sentimental paper to the boxes at fun angles.

5. Cut out three musical notes or other fun shapes from the watercolor paper. Use rubber stamps to color the edges of the cutout shapes. Let them dry.

6. Write song lyrics on plain paper. Cut them out with decorative-edge scissors.

7. Glue the song lyric strips to the card stock boxes. Then use alphabet stickers or stencils to call out a word from the lyrics on each square.

8. Cut 12 strips from scrap paper that are ¼x2 inches (.6x5 cm). Glue the ends of two strips together to form two sides of a square. Fold the strips back and forth over each other to form a springy column. Repeat with the other strips.

9. Glue four columns to the back of one paper shape. Glue the other ends of the columns to a card stock box. The paper shape will float a bit above the box. Repeat with the other shapes.

10. Cut a 31-inch (79-cm) piece of ribbon. Hot glue the boxes to the ribbon, leaving 1 inch (2.5 cm) between each box and 4 inches (10 cm) at the top and bottom. Fold the top and bottom ribbon ends over into loops and hot glue in place.

Materials:

3 7-inch (18-cm) squares of patterned card stock

craft knife

invisible tape

craft glue

3 5-inch (13-cm) squares cut from sentimental paper such as concert programs or flyers

heavy watercolor paper

rubber stamps and ink pad

permanent marker

plain paper

decorative-edge scissors

alphabet stickers or stencils

4-inch (10-cm) wide ribbon

hot glue

Captivating Container

With a few petals from a dance corsage or a nature walk, this bowl will hold your makeup—and your memories.

1. Rip the construction paper into tiny pieces and put them in a large bowl. Pour in just enough water to cover the paper. Mix it with your hand to be sure that all the paper gets wet. Let the mixture sit at least eight hours.

2. Pour the paper and water mixture into a blender and blend until smooth pulp forms. Pour the mixture into a bowl.

3. Grab a handful of pulp. Squeeze water out of the pulp over an empty bowl. Squeeze until the pulp is as wet as a damp sponge. Place the pulp in a clean bowl. Repeat with the rest of the pulp.

4. Add the salt, glitter, craft glue, and flowers to the bowl of pulp. Use your hands to gently mix everything together.

5. Cover the inside of a small bowl with petroleum jelly. Smooth a layer of plastic wrap over the jelly, with enough extra to fold over the edges of the bowl. Smooth another layer of petroleum jelly over the plastic.

6. Line strips of tissue paper inside the bowl to make stripes. Use as many or as few as you'd like. Trim the strips so they don't overlap the edge.

7. Press the paper pulp into the bowl over the tissue paper. Keep pressing the pulp into the bowl until the whole bowl is covered. Smooth the edge of the paper pulp by gently pinching it.

8. To make a colored lip on your bowl, press tissue paper strips along the paper pulp's edge. Gently fold the paper around the edge of the paper pulp. Use a fingernail or knife to tuck it between the pulp and the plastic wrap.

9. Let your bowl dry for three to four days. When it is completely dry, pull on the plastic wrap to release your bowl from the mold. Peel the plastic wrap off your bowl.

10. Brush decoupage glue over the entire bowl. Let it dry completely. Repeat two more times.

Materials:

four pieces of construction paper

water

1 teaspoon (5 mL) salt

2 teaspoons (10 mL) glitter

¼ cup (60 mL) craft glue

¼ cup (60 mL) flower petals or small flowers

3- to 4-inch (8- to 10-cm) wide bowl to use as a mold

petroleum jelly

plastic wrap

brightly colored tissue paper, cut into ¼-inch (.6-cm) strips

foam brush

decoupage glue

Tip: For a smoother bowl, use toilet paper instead of construction paper.

Timeline Journal

Time flies when you're having fun. Remember all the details of a special event with this unique journal.

1. Lay one piece of cardboard on the wrapping paper. Wrap the cardboard like a gift, then unfold. Brush decoupage glue on both sides of the cardboard. Lay the cardboard back on the wrapping paper and refold. Secure the ends of the paper with glue if needed. Repeat with the other cardboard piece.

2. Lay the drawing paper out on your workspace. Fold the left-hand side over 5 inches (13 cm) and crease. Then fold that section under 5 inches (13-cm) and crease. Continue to accordion fold the paper until you reach the end.

3. Unfold the drawing paper stack and lay it out on your workspace. Draw a straight line 4 inches (10 cm) from the bottom across the length of the paper, stopping at the crease just before the last section.

4. On the left-hand side, write the first date of a special trip or other event along the line you drew. Glue photos, newspaper clippings, or other paper souvenirs around the date. Write any notes or comments you have on the page too. Continue adding dates and memories to the pages in the order they occurred. Leave the last 5-inch (13-cm) section of paper blank. When done, refold the paper. When folded, the top of the stack should be blank.

Materials:

2 9x5½-inch (23x14-cm) pieces of cardboard

wrapping paper

foam brush

decoupage glue

8½x50-inch (22x127-cm) piece of drawing paper, cut from a roll

permanent markers

glue stick

photos and other paper souvenirs from a special event

2 9x5½-inch (23x14-cm) pieces of tissue paper in two different colors

alphabet stickers

3½x 5½-inch (9x14-cm) piece of vellum

hot glue

additional embellishments, such as extra vellum, stick-on decorations, flowers, or ribbon

5. Apply glue to the blank front page of the folded paper stack. Lay one decorated cardboard piece on top of the glue and press gently.

6. Turn the stack over and apply glue to the bottom page. Attach the second cardboard piece to this glued page. Turn the project back over.

7. Brush decoupage on the front cover. Lay a piece of tissue paper on the glue. Brush more glue over the paper and cover it with a second piece of tissue. Let dry.

8. Use alphabet stickers to put a title for your journal on the piece of vellum. Hot glue the vellum to the cardboard cover. If wanted, decorate the front cover with other vellum cutouts, tissue paper, stick-on elements, flowers, or ribbons.

Locket of Love

Keep those you love close to your heart. Craft this lovely locket from paper, and fill it with a picture you can treasure every day.

1. Use a heart-shaped paper punch to cut two hearts from card stock and one from a photo. (Or trace a heart-shaped cookie cutter and cut them out by hand.)

2. Stick two paper reinforcement rings together. Glue the ring to the top left of one of the paper hearts. Half of the reinforcement should hang over the edge. Repeat for the top right and middle of the heart.

3. Glue the photo over the paper heart and reinforcements.

4. Cut the other paper heart in half from top to bottom.

5. Turn the heart with the photo upside down. Brush the back of this heart with decoupage glue. Apply glue to both sides of the heart halves too.

6. Cut a 6-inch (15-cm) piece of ribbon. Glue the ribbon to the back of one heart half near the straight edge. Put the ribbon at the same height as the reinforcement rings on the photo heart. Repeat for the other heart half.

7. Cut two ¼x1-inch (.6x2.5-cm) strips and two ¼x ½-inch (.6x1-cm) strips from scrap paper. Fold one strip in half. Then fold each end back to the fold. When you lay the paper on its side, it should look like a W. Repeat with the other strips.

Materials:

2-inch (5-cm) wide heart-shaped paper punch or small heart cookie cutter

card stock

photo

¼-inch (.6-cm) paper reinforcement rings

craft glue

foam brush

decoupage glue

thin ribbon

scrap paper

clear, dimensional paper sealant

paper hole punch

decorative paper

Tip: Always let the glue dry before moving on to the next step.

8. Cover the photo with dimensional paper sealant. While it is still wet, place the short paper strips on the bottom left and right of the photo. Place the longer paper strips on the top left and right of the photo. Attach each strip only up to the first fold. Pop any air bubbles in the sealant with a toothpick.

9. Glue the ends of the strips to the split hearts so that the heart pieces close over the photo.

10. Thread the ribbon from the left heart piece through the left reinforcement ring. Repeat on the right. Tie the ribbons together at the back of the locket. When you pull on the ribbon, the heart halves will slide open to reveal the photo underneath.

11. Punch out small circles from the decorative paper. Glue them to the heart halves as decoration.

12. Thread a 20-inch (51-cm) piece of ribbon through the ring at the top of the heart. Knot the ends together.

Photo Ornament

Friends are forever with this keepsake ornament. It will be a treasured reminder of your bond for years to come.

Materials:

1½-inch (4-cm) circle paper punch
or a small can for tracing

decorative scrapbook paper in three
different colors or designs

glue stick

10-inch (25-cm) string or ribbon

needle

½-inch (1-cm) circle paper punch
or a nickel for tracing

photos of friends

1. Using your 1½-inch (4-cm) paper punch, cut out seven circles from each of the different scrapbook papers. (You can also cut your circles by hand, using a small can for tracing.)

2. Take one of the circles and write a "T" for template on it. This circle won't be used in the actual ornament. Fold the edges of your template toward the center to make a triangle. The corners of the triangle should be on the edge of the circle. All three sides should be the same length. (This might take a few tries.)

3. Place each of the circles on the template. Fold the circles, using the template as a guide.

4. Glue 10 triangles to each other in a straight line by their folded tabs. The points and bases of the triangles will alternate. Make the line into a ring by gluing the last triangle to the first at the side tabs.

5. To make the top of the ornament, glue five triangles together side by side, with all of the points facing up. Do the same with the last five triangles to make the bottom. You should have two domes.

6. Glue the five remaining tabs on the top dome to the five tabs on the top of the ring.

7. Thread a ribbon through a needle. Start the needle inside the ball and poke it up through a corner in the dome. Then pass the ribbon back down into the dome to make a loop on the top of the ornament. Tie the ribbon ends in a knot, and glue the knot to the inside of the ball.

8. Glue the remaining dome to the bottom of the ring, as in step 6.

9. Use a ½-inch (1-cm) circle punch to cut circles from the photos. (You can also cut these circles by hand, using a nickel for tracing.) Glue these photo circles in as many of the ornament segments as you like. Let dry.

Party Scrapbook

Some parties you never want to forget.
After your bash, reuse the gift wrap
and ribbons to make this scrapbook.
It will be like holding your party
in your hands.

1. Cut 10 4½x6-inch (11x15-cm) pieces from card stock. Cut two pieces of the same size from cardboard.

2. Use a piece of wrapping paper to cover the top half of one cardboard piece. Fold the paper over the edges to cover both sides, and trim the paper as needed. Unfold. Do the same with a different piece of wrapping paper on the bottom half of the piece and unfold.

3. Brush decoupage glue over both sides of the cardboard piece. Rewrap the wrapping papers around the piece. Cover the seam with a length of ribbon, secured with craft glue.

4. Repeat steps 2–3 with the other cardboard piece.

5. Punch five holes through the cardboard pieces, ½ inch (1 cm) from the left edge. Do the same with the card stock pages.

6. Decorate one cardboard piece with more ribbons, punched pieces from greeting cards, and other elements that fit your party's theme. This will be the book's front cover.

7. Fill the inside pages with photos, stickers, and other souvenirs from the party. Write details about the party on the pages too, so you'll never forget the fun you had!

8. Stack the front cover, pages, and back cover together so the holes align.

9. Thread a 28-inch (71-cm) piece of ribbon through the bottom holes of the book. Make the ribbon ends even, then tie a knot at the spine of the book.

10. Lace the ribbon up the book's spine, ending with a double-knotted bow. Glue beads or charms to the ends of the ribbon if desired.

Materials:

solid color card stock

cardboard

wrapping paper from a party

foam brush

decoupage glue

ribbon from a party

craft glue

paper hole punch

greeting cards from a party

stick-on paper embellishments to suit your theme

photos and other paper souvenirs from a party

beads or charms (optional)

Tip: When binding your book, use binder clips to keep the pages lined up.

Keepsake Box

Special treasures deserve a special home. Create a keepsake box that's as pretty as the things you put inside.

1. Turn the box lid upside down on a piece of copy paper. Trace around the lid. Set this paper aside.

2. Turn the lid right-side up. Lay a strip of tissue paper on the lid. Brush decoupage glue over the strip, smoothing the wrinkles. Continue adding paper until the lid and its sides are covered. Trim pieces that go past the edges. Allow the lid to dry.

3. Cut decorative paper to fit around the outside of the box. Brush decoupage glue on the box and attach the paper.

4. Inside the lid tracing, draw a design for the top of your box. Keep at least ⅛ inch (.3 cm) of space between all the lines.

5. Place your drawing on a cutting mat. Use a craft knife to cut out the picture you drew. If you accidentally cut off a section, tape the pieces back together and keep going. This will be your stencil.

6. Attach the stencil to patterned paper with repositionable tape.

7. Place the stencil and paper on the cutting mat. Use your stencil to guide you as you cut out your design from the patterned paper. Don't worry if you accidentally cut too far or tear the paper. You can repair it later.

8. Gently remove the stencil and tape from the cut out design.

9. Brush a thin layer of decoupage glue on the lid. Carefully press your cut paper on the lid. If any parts of the design were torn or cut off, use the brush and glue to fix the damage. Gently smooth out any wrinkles.

10. Brush three layers of decoupage glue over the paper cutting, allowing the glue to dry between coats.

Materials:

small cardboard or paper mache box with lid

copy paper

tissue paper cut into strips

foam brush

decoupage glue

decorative paper

self-healing cutting mat or piece of corrugated cardboard

craft knife

repositionable tape

Tips: If you need to cut out a clean point, cut toward the point from both sides. Don't try to turn the corner.

Don't try to cut all the way through the paper the first time. Instead, work on getting the line right. Then go over it again.

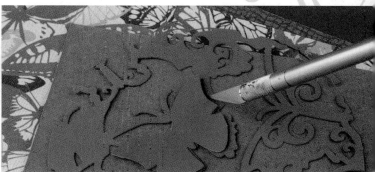

Time Capsule

Freeze a moment in time with this paper craft project. Fill the time capsule with mementos from this year, then stash it away to rediscover years from now.

Materials:

metallic papers

cylindrical mailer or poster tube

craft glue

old calendar pages

alphabet stickers

other stickers or small paper
cut-outs (optional)

2-inch (5-cm) circle paper punch
or a can for tracing

paper hole punch

thin ribbon

1. Cut a piece of metallic paper the length and circumference of the tube. If your tube has a cap that comes down over the top, cut a piece to cover the cap too.

2. Glue the paper around the tube and cap.

3. Cut words and dates from an old calendar. Glue them around the tube to form borders.

4. Use alphabet stickers to spell the words "Time Capsule" and the year on the center of the tube.

5. Use other stickers or shape cut-outs to decorate the tube, if desired.

6. Use your paper punch to cut out two circles from metallic paper. (You can also cut your circles by hand, using a can for tracing.)

7. Use stickers or a marker to put "Do not open until" on one circle. Put a year for opening your time capsule on the other circle.

8. Punch a hole on the edge of each circle. Tie the circles together with ribbon.

9. Glue the ribbon around the top of the time capsule, letting the circles dangle.

10. Put mementos from the year, predictions, and written memories inside your time capsule. Put it someplace safe until it's time to open it!

Initially Quilled

Special events color your life. Let the programs or flyers from those events color your room. This decoration uses a paper craft skill called quilling. It might take some time to master, but the results will be well worth it.

1. Cut your flyers or programs into ⅛-inch (.3-cm) wide strips. A paper cutter or paper shredder make quick work of this. But you can use a ruler and scissors too.

2. In a word processing program, type the letter you want to quill. Enlarge the letter so it fills the page. Print it out, and cut out the letter. This is your stencil.

3. Trace the stencil onto the center of the card stock.

4. Place a line of glue around the outline of the letter. Hold a paper strip on its edge. Curve and bend it along the lines to create a "wall" around the letter. Hold it in place until it's set. Continue building paper walls around the entire letter. Let dry.

5. Squeeze a small puddle of glue onto scrap paper.

Materials:

flyers or programs from a special event

8½x11-inch (22x28-cm) piece of solid color card stock

craft glue

slotted quilling tool

quilling needle

tweezers

mat board with an 8½x11-inch (22x28-cm) opening

picture frame to fit the mat board

6. Insert a paper strip into the slotted quilling tool. Hold the tool with your dominant hand, and rest the tool on your other hand's forefinger. Roll the tool to quill the paper. When you get to the end, hold the rolled strip securely using your thumb and middle finger. Push the paper roll off the tool.

7. Use the quilling needle to apply glue to the rolled paper end. Press and hold until secure.

8. Grab the quilled shape with tweezers, and dip the bottom edges in glue. Place the shape inside the walls of the letter.

9. Continue filling in the letter with quilled shapes, allowing some tails of paper to curl up off the paper for a 3-D effect. Let the project dry completely.

10. Place the mat board over the project, and then frame for a finished look.

Flowering Friends

Give your space flair with these scented photo flowers. You'll have plenty of room for all your buds.

1. On card stock, draw and cut out a flower petal that measures 2 inches (5 cm) long, 2 inches (5 cm) at the widest part, and ¾ inch (2 cm) wide at the bottom. This is your template.

2. Use your template to trace seven petals onto the back of one sheet of decorative paper. Then cut out the petals.

3. Fold one petal in half the long way, pattern side out. Accordion fold each edge to the center fold. Repeat on the rest of the petals.

4. From a different piece of decorative paper, punch a 1-inch (2.5-cm) circle and a 2-inch (5-cm) circle.

5. Punch a 1½-inch (4-cm) circle from a photo.

6. Squeeze hot glue onto the center of the 1-inch (2.5-cm) circle. Arrange the petals evenly around the circle, with the small ends in the hot glue. Flatten the petals slightly.

7. Squeeze hot glue on the back side of the 2-inch (5-cm) circle. Press it on top of the flower where the petals come together. Then glue the photo circle to this circle.

8. Repeat steps 2–7 to create as many flowers as you'd like.

9. Hot glue the flowers onto branches. Arrange the branches in a pail or vase filled with sand or pebbles.

10. Spritz the backs of your flowers with a summerlike scent that reminds you of your friends.

Materials:

scrap piece of card stock

decorative paper in several different colors or patterns

1-inch (2.5-cm), 1½-inch (4-cm), and 2-inch (5-cm) circle paper punches (or small round objects for tracing)

photos of friends

hot glue

dry tree branches

large pail or vase

sand or pebbles

perfume

Expanding Idea Book

Have an idea you don't want to forget?
Need a place to jot down things to do?
Use this handy book for all your notes,
and you'll always have a record of how
far you've come.

1. Glue one of the decorative papers to one cardboard piece. The paper should overhang the cardboard by ½ inch (1 cm) on every side. Fold the overhanging paper over the edges and glue to the back of the cardboard.

2. Glue an index card to the back of the cardboard over the paper edges.

3. Repeat steps 1–2 with the second piece of cardboard and paper.

4. Stick the adhesive cork to the front of one cardboard piece. Use decorative-edge scissors to cut a square from scrap paper. Write a title on the paper, and glue the paper to the cork. Decorate the cork with pins, tacks and other office supplies.

5. Punch holes in the front and back covers ½ inch (1 cm) from the top edge and 1 inch (2.5 cm) from the left and right edges. Punch holes in the same locations on your index cards, using the front cover as a guide.

6. Lay a piece of packing tape across the bottom edge of one index card, extending the tape 1 inch (2.5 cm) out from the right edge. Fold the tape back on itself to make a tab.

7. Use decorative-edge scissors to cut a small label from scrap paper. Write a category title on it. Glue the label to the packing tape tab.

8. Repeat steps 6–7 to make other category pages. Shift the place where you put the tape so that each tab sticks out in a different place on the right edge of the card.

9. Load the back cover, index cards, category pages, and front cover onto the two book rings. Close the rings.

10. Start filling those index cards with reminders, notes, recipes, and lists!

Materials:

craft glue

2 5x7-inch (13x18-cm) pieces of decorative paper

2 4x6-inch (10x15-cm) pieces of cardboard

20–30 4x6-inch (10x15-cm) index cards

3x5-inch (8x13-cm) sheet of adhesive cork

decorative-edge scissors

scrap paper

permanent marker

pins, tacks, or other decorations for the cover

paper hole punch

printed packing tape

2 1-inch (2.5-cm) metal book rings

Tips: If you fill up all the index cards, just open the rings and add more!

Newspaper Basket

Snag a copy of the Sunday paper, and weave this unique basket. It's a perfect decoration for a living room, plus it keeps things organized!

1. Trim off the newspaper folds so you have single pages.

2. Fold each page into a long strip that is about 1½ inches (4 cm) wide.

3. Put two strips side by side on your workspace horizontally. Weave a third strip over and under the middle of the first strips. Glue the third strip in place.

4. Weave three more strips on the left side of the vertical strip. Then weave four strips on the right side of the vertical strip. Make sure the strips are close together. Glue the strips in place.

5. Turn the project so the horizontal strips are vertical. Then weave in six more strips so you have a total of eight in the center. Make sure these are close together too. Glue the strips in place. This will be the bottom of the basket.

6. Fold the leftover stripping up to shape the side frames. It's OK if they don't all stand up on their own. They will later.

7. Glue one paper strip end to a corner along the bottom of one side. Weave the strip horizontally along the bottom, going in and out of the strips you folded up to make the frame. Glue the strip to the frame as you work to keep it from sliding. When you reach a corner, pinch the strips together to make a corner angle.

When you reach the end of the strip, glue another strip to it and continue weaving until you reach the corner where you started. Trim off any excess paper and glue the ends together.

8. Repeat step 7 two or three more times. Your sides will have three or four rows, depending on how tall you want the basket to be.

9. Fold excess frame strips over so they lay flat on the inside. Staple the top of each top strip. Trim away the extra paper below the staples.

10. Glue ribbon around the basket's top to hide the staples and give the basket a finished look.

Silhouette Tree

Assemble a unique family tree, complete with pets and friends, to decorate your home. A wall makes a spectacular canvas.

Materials:

wood patterned or brown shelf liner

photos

construction paper

decorative papers

glue stick

masking tape

1. On the back side of the shelf liner, draw a tree trunk that is 24 inches (61 cm) tall or taller. Then draw branches and leaves in the sizes and shapes you want. Cut out the shapes. Peel off the paper backing and attach your tree to a wall.

2. Cut out the subject of a photo. Cut carefully so you don't lose the little details.

3. Trace the cut photo onto construction paper. Cut out the silhouette.

4. Cut a piece of decorative paper into a fun shape, such as an oval, star, or house. Make this shape large enough that the silhouette can fit on top.

5. On a different piece of paper, cut a larger version of the shape you cut in step 4.

6. Glue the smaller shape to the larger shape. Then glue the silhouette on top.

7. Repeat steps 2–6 to create several other silhouette pictures.

8. Attach the silhouette pictures to the tree with hidden squares of masking tape.

Tip: Choose photos that have fun details, such as wisps of hair, curly tails, or noses. Profile photos work best.

Bookshelf Zoo

Give your book collection some character with these crazy creatures.

1. On a piece of copy paper, draw the animal you want to make. If drawing isn't your thing, do an Internet search for animal templates. Print off one you like.

2. Cut out your drawing or template.

3. Trace the template onto a piece of patterned card stock. Then trace it again on a piece of solid color card stock. Cut out each shape.

4. Glue the patterned animal piece to the solid color animal. Make sure the solid color piece peeks out from behind the patterned piece. This will create a 3D effect.

5. If you wish, enhance a feature on the animal. For example, give it a set of wiggly eyes or paint glitter on a tail.

6. Repeat steps 1–5 for a whole zoo.

Tip: Label the animals with letters from the alphabet or book categories to make organizing your books fun and easy.

Paper Lanterns

Light up a room with this simple but classy decoration. Fun shapes will dance across your walls, and you'll dance with enjoyment.

1. Cut two strips 1½ inches (4 cm) wide by 8 inches (20 cm) long from a piece of origami paper.

2. With the pattern side down, form an X with the strips. Glue the strips together where they intersect. The square in the middle of the X will be the bottom of the box.

3. Fold one arm of the X so the outside edge meets the closest edge of the bottom square. Crease the paper so it makes a crisp line. Then fold the square arm over so it lies on top of the bottom square. Crease this fold well too. Unfold.

4. Repeat step 3 with the other three strips.

5. On a protected surface, use a craft knife to cut a small X in the bottom square.

6. Use paper punches to punch out fun designs in each arm of the X. Be careful not to punch holes on the creases.

7. Assemble the box by folding two side strips up on the creases to form a top square. Glue these pieces together. Then fold up the next two sides to join the top square. Glue them all together. Let dry.

8. Repeat steps 1–7 to make enough boxes to cover each light on the string.

9. Before hanging, gently push an LED light through the X in the bottom of each box.

Materials:

8-inch (20-cm) origami paper squares

craft glue

craft knife

paper punches in fun shapes

string of LED lights

Tip: These boxes can light up any time of year. Use holiday-themed papers to decorate for a special event. Or use papers that coordinate with your room for everyday decor.

Colorful Coverlet

Don't leave your bed out of the decorating fun. Add a splash of color to any bedroom with this patchwork paper project.

1. Mix 2 teaspoons (10 mL) of dye with ½ cup (120 mL) of water in a glass or metal bowl. Submerge two paper sheets in the colored water and soak for at least five minutes. Wearing rubber gloves, gently squeeze excess water from the sheets. Place them on newspaper covered with paper towels to dry. Smooth out any wrinkles.

2. Repeat step 1 to dye all the paper sheets. You'll need to dye 20 sheets with one color. Dye six sheets a second color, six sheets a third color, and eight sheets a fourth color.

3. Assemble the dyed blocks according to the pattern shown below. Start with the left column. Put a thin line of hot glue on the long edge of a block. Overlap the long edge of a second block ½ inch (1 cm), and gently press down. Smooth with your finger. Make sure the edges match up and the seams face the same direction as you continue assembling the column. Let dry.

4. Repeat step 3 to create a total of five columns.

5. Attach the columns to each other by running a thin line of hot glue along the edge of a column. Press a second column on top, overlapping ½ inch (1 cm). Let dry well.

6. Take your coverlet to a dry but well-ventilated space. Follow the directions on the can to apply water-resistant sealant.

Materials:

four complementary food dye colors

40 8½x11-inch (22x28-cm) white quilt block foundation non-woven paper sheets

rubber gloves

newspaper and paper towels

hot glue

clear acrylic gloss coating sealant

Tip: This project covers a standard twin bed. If you have a larger bed, double the number of paper sheets and make 10 columns.

Coverlet Pattern

Color 1	Color 1	Color 1	Color 1	Color 1
Color 1	Color 4	Color 2	Color 4	Color 1
Color 2	Color 1	Color 3	Color 1	Color 2
Color 4	Color 3	Color 1	Color 3	Color 4
Color 2	Color 3	Color 1	Color 3	Color 2
Color 4	Color 1	Color 3	Color 1	Color 4
Color 1	Color 4	Color 2	Color 4	Color 1
Color 1	Color 1	Color 1	Color 1	Color 1

Sassy Sachet

Don't just make your place look good. Make it smell good too! You'll actually use a common kitchen paper product to make these perfect pillows.

Materials:

food dye colors or tea bag

flat bottom (basket style)
coffee filters

paper towels

stencils

thin tipped markers

glue stick

potpourri

1. Mix at least 6 drops of dye with ¼ cup (60 mL) of water in a bowl. For an earthy brown dye, use the tea bag to brew a mug of tea. Let it completely cool, and then pour ¼ cup (60 mL) into a bowl.

2. Flatten a coffee filter so it is a large round circle. Soak it in the dye for at least five minutes.

3. Carefully squeeze the excess water from the filter. Spread the filter on paper towels to dry. They will take a couple of hours to dry.

4. Fold two sides of the filter so they touch in the middle. Fold up the bottom half and then fold down the top half to form flaps of an envelope.

5. Unfold the flaps and turn the filter over. The fold lines show what will be the front of the envelope.

6. On a protected surface, stencil a pattern on the front of the envelope. The markers will bleed through a bit.

7. Turn the envelope back over, refold the sides and bottom flaps. Glue the bottom to the sides. Fill the envelope with potpourri. Glue down the top flap.

8. Repeat steps 1–7 to make as many sachets as you want.

Crafty Creatures

Make your friends hoot and roar with laughter with these silly decorations. And you can store treasures in the jars hidden underneath.

1. Cut a strip of decorative paper 3 inches (8 cm) tall and 9 inches (23 cm) wide. Brush glue on a jar. Wrap the paper around the jar so the top edge is flush against the jar's bottom lip. Hold the paper in place to dry. Repeat with an orange strip of paper and the second jar.

2. Cut a strip of patterned paper 3 inches (8 cm) tall and 10 inches (25 cm) wide. Fold the strip in half, patterned side facing out. Fold each side of the strip inward toward the center fold. Wrap the strip around the top of the blue jar. One fold should face the front and the other folds will be on either side. Glue the back edges together to fit snuggly around the jar. Repeat with orange paper to make the lion's head.

3. Cut two 3½x1-inch (9x2.5-cm) strips and two 4½x1-inch (11x2.5-cm) strips from orange paper. Glue these strips together to make a frame with the longer strips on the top and bottom. Snip a ragged fringe around the outside edges of the frame. Glue the mane to the lion's head.

4. Use a stencil to draw two small ovals on a piece of white paper. Cut out the shapes. Cut out whiskers and a mouth from black paper. Punch out five small circles from the black paper too. Then cut out a nose shape from red paper.

5. Glue the ovals to the lion's face as eyes. Use black circles to create pupils. Glue on the other facial features too. Glue the other black circles to the body like buttons.

6. For the owl, cut two chunky rectangles from black paper. Snip the rectangles into strips for the wings. Cut a rectangle with one pointy end from patterned paper for a necktie. Cut out two small circles from white paper. Cut two half circles and one triangle from orange paper. Punch out two small circles from black paper.

Materials:

decorative paper in several colors, including orange, white, black, and red

foam brush

craft glue

2 half-pint jelly jars

shape stencils

paper hole punch

7. Glue the white circles to the owl as eyes. Use the black circles to create pupils. Glue the orange half circles on top of the white circles as eyelids. Fold the triangle in half. Align the crease with the crease in the head and glue in place. Glue on the wings and necktie too.

8. Cut out four large ovals from orange paper. Glue two ovals to the bottom of each jar as feet.

Letter Lineup

Showcase your personality with cardboard letters featuring papers you love. Try using unusual papers such as maps, photographs, comics, animal prints, or old homework. Make these letters spell YOU!

Materials:

several pieces of thick corrugated cardboard

craft knife

craft glue

decorative papers in a variety of prints and colors

glue stick

foam brush

decoupage glue

1. Using a word processing program, type the letter you want to make. Enlarge the font so the letter fills the whole page. Print it, then cut out your letter. This is your template.

2. Trace the template onto at least two pieces of cardboard. The more cardboard pieces you use, the thicker your finished project will be.

3. Lay one cardboard piece on a protected surface. Use a craft knife to cut out the letter. Repeat with the other cardboard pieces.

4. Stack the letters, using craft glue between each piece to keep them together.

5. Trace your template on a piece of decorative paper. Then turn the template over, and trace it on another piece of decorative paper. Cut out both letters.

6. Use the glue stick to attach the decorative paper to the front and back of the cardboard letter stack.

7. Measure the side width of your letter and the length around the letter edges. Cut out strips of decorative paper in these dimensions. To make this step easier, cut short strips and overlap the edges as you wind around the letter. Attach the strips with the glue stick.

8. Brush decoupage glue over the entire letter for a finished look. Let dry.

9. Repeat steps 1–8 to make as many letters as you need.

Tip: When cutting the cardboard, start with light cuts to make an outline. Then apply more pressure to cut through the layers.

Dot Art

Dot your room with a colorful display. Papers punched into tiny circles can make a surprising decoration when pieced together one by one.

8½x11-inch (22x28-cm) sheet of white card stock

double-sided reusable cling sheets

paper dots of assorted colors

tweezers

picture frame

1. Lightly sketch the picture you want to make on the card stock. It might help to sketch the drawing on copy paper first to avoid too many errors on the card stock.

2. Attach cling sheets to the card stock, filling the whole page. Trim away anything that hangs over the edge of the card stock.

3. Organize the paper dots into color piles.

4. Remove the clear protective film from the tops of the cling sheets. Start creating your picture on the sticky surface one dot at a time. Fill the entire paper so only small portions of the card stock shows through. If you make a mistake, simply use tweezers to move the dots as needed.

5. When you're done, frame your artwork for display.

Tip: Tired of your picture? No problem. Just remove the dots from the adhesive surface and wipe it with a damp cloth. Let the surface dry before starting over.

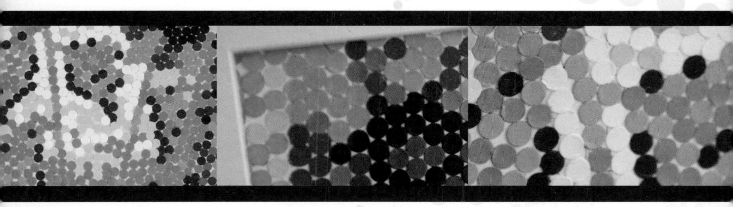

Picture Perfect Lamp

**Take a lamp from plain to perfect just by adding paper!
Use papers you love, and let your style shine through.**

any paper you love, such as sheet music, magazines, maps, or posters

flat-sided lamp shade

glue stick

foam brush

decoupage glue

1. Cut shapes out of your papers. You could cut images from magazines, music note shapes from sheet music, or funky shapes from funky paper.

2. Decide how to arrange your images or shapes on the lamp shade. Once you're certain of the design, use the glue stick to attach the pictures.

3. Carefully brush decoupage glue over the entire lamp shade. Let dry. Then apply a second coat and let dry.

Tip: Look for bargain lamp shades at your local thrift store or garage sales. Just make sure they're in good shape and clean them when you get home.

Stacked Jewelry Box Tree

Keep your jewelry organized and decorate your room at the same time with these decorated paper boxes.

1. In a well-ventilated area, spray paint three of the boxes inside and out. Also paint the paper mache box. Let dry. Keep the other three boxes and the lid white.

2. Punch paper circles from decorative papers. You probably need at least 70 circles.

3. Use the glue stick to attach dots to all six jewelry boxes and the lid. You can put them in straight rows or mix it up. It's up to you!

4. Brush decoupage glue over all of the jewelry boxes inside and out. Let them dry.

5. Working on a protected surface, use a craft knife to make two ½-inch (1-cm) cuts in the bottom of each box. Make the cuts in an X near the middle of one of the long edges.

6. Turn the paper mache box upside down. Cut a similar X in the center of this box.

7. Slide the boxes onto the dowel through the Xs, and arrange them as you like.

8. Push the bottom end of the dowel into the X in the paper mache box. Fill around the dowel with craft glue to keep it in place. Let dry.

9. Use the craft knife to cut a small X in the middle of the lid. Brush craft glue on the bottom of the button, and gently push the shank through the X so the button sits against the lid. Let dry.

10. Set the lid on top of the jewelry box tree.

Materials:

glossy craft spray paint

6 2x3-inch (5x8-cm) white cardboard jewelry boxes and one lid

4-inch (10-cm) square paper mache box

paper hole punch

decorative paper

glue stick

foam brush

glossy decoupage glue

craft knife

³⁄₁₆x9-inch (.5x23-cm) wooden dowel

craft glue

large button with shank

Garland Wind Chime

Fill your home with music, or at least a few bells. These pretty heart chimes are a decoration that will be music to your ears.

Materials:

reversible wrapping paper

glue stick

paper hole punch

colored paper clips

three small bells

thin ribbon

1. Cut five strips, each 1½ inches (4 cm) wide, from wrapping paper. Make two strips 10 inches (25 cm) long, two strips 8 inches (20 cm) long, and one strip 6¾ inches (17 cm) long.

2. Punch a hole about ½ inch (1 cm) from one short edge of the shortest strip.

3. Lay the short strip on your work space, punched hole at the top. Lay an 8-inch (20-cm) strip on top of the short strip with the bottom edges aligned. Glue the bottom edges together.

4. Bend the top edge of the longer strip down into a half heart shape. Glue the edge to the short strip 1½ inches (4 cm) below the hole.

5. Align the bottom edge of a 10-inch (25-cm) strip with the bottom of the heart half. Glue the edges together. Bend the strip around the first heart half to make a second heart half. Tuck the top edge between the short strip and the first heart half, and glue in place.

6. Repeat steps 3–5 on the other side of the short strip.

7. Punch a hole through the glued bottom edges about ½ inch (1 cm) from the edge.

8. Put the open end of a paper clip through the back hook of each bell. Push the bells around the clip to secure. Thread the paper clip through the bottom hole.

9. Thread a paper clip through the top hole. Pull a length of ribbon through the paper clip to create a hanger.

Quilled Paper Candle Sleeve

Add a soft, warm glow to any room with this beautiful glowing decoration. Quilled paper designs wrapped around a flameless candle will add just the spark you need.

Materials:

wax paper

flameless candle

quilling paper strips

slotted quilling tool

quilling needle

craft glue

tweezers

double-stick tape

1. Cut wax paper so it will wrap around the candle like a sleeve that fits snugly but can be slipped on and off. Add 2 inches (5 cm) to the height so the paper will be taller than the candle.

2. Insert a quilling strip into the slotted quilling tool. Hold the tool with your dominant hand, and rest the tool on your other hand's forefinger. Roll the tool to quill the paper. When you get to the end, hold the rolled strip securely using your thumb and middle finger. Push the paper roll off the tool.

3. Using the quilling needle, apply glue to the rolled paper end. Press and hold until secure.

4. Repeat steps 2–3 to create several rolled strips. Be creative with the shapes, using the quilling techniques below.

5. Lay the cut wax paper on a table and position your shapes. Pour a bit of glue onto a piece of scratch paper. Grab a quilled shape with tweezers and gently dip the bottom edges in the glue. Set the shape on the paper, and hold it down with your finger until the glue sets. Repeat with all the shapes.

6. Tape the seams of the sleeve together once your design is finished. Slip the sleeve over the candle.

Quilling Techniques

Glue together different colored strips before quilling to create larger shapes of more than one color.

Cut the paper strips shorter to create smaller shapes.

To create more openness within a shape, roll the paper strip tightly. Then loosen up your fingers a bit to get the look you want before gluing down the edge.

To create a square, roll the paper strip into a circle. Then use both hands to pinch all sides inward at the same time.

To create a leaf, roll the paper strip into a circle. Then pinch two ends at the same time.

To create a teardrop shape, roll the paper strip into a circle and pinch one end.

Creature Calendar

Don't let important dates crawl up on you. Keep life organized and fun with this cute caterpillar calendar.